OPENING YOUR FIRST ROBINHOOD ACCOUNT

A BEGINNER'S JOURNEY

This book is for informational and educational purposes only. The author and publisher do not provide financial, legal, or investment advice. While every effort has been made to ensure the accuracy of the information, the author assumes no responsibility for any decisions made based on the content of this book. Readers are encouraged to research and consult a qualified professional before making financial or investment decisions.

First Edition

TABLE OF CONTENTS

Chapter 1: Introduction to Robinhood

Overview of the Robinhood App

The Robinhood app has transformed how individuals approach investing by providing a user-friendly platform for novice and experienced traders. Launched in 2013, Robinhood broke down barriers to entry into the financial markets by offering commission-free trading. This innovative approach democratized access to stock trading. It paved the way for a younger generation to engage with financial instruments and cryptocurrencies without the traditional fees associated with brokerage services. The app's intuitive design and easy navigation make it an attractive option for anyone over 18 looking to start investing.

Safety and security are paramount concerns for users when selecting a trading platform. Robinhood employs industry-standard encryption to protect personal and financial information while using the app. Additionally, the platform is a member of the Financial Industry Regulatory Authority (FINRA) and the Securities Investor Protection Corporation (SIPC), which provides users with up to $500,000 in protection for their securities, including a $250,000 limit for cash claims. These measures ensure that accounts are safeguarded against unauthorized access and potential financial loss, instilling confidence in new traders.

Trading on Robinhood is designed to be straightforward, whether users buy stocks, ETFs, or cryptocurrencies. The app allows easy access to real-time market data, enabling users to make informed trading decisions. Robinhood offers cryptocurrency enthusiasts a simplified way to trade popular digital currencies like Bitcoin and Ethereum without incurring traditional transaction fees. This accessibility encourages users to explore various financial instruments, allowing them to diversify their portfolios and engage with different asset classes.

Transferring funds to and from ACH accounts is a critical feature of the Robinhood app. Users can link their bank accounts for seamless deposits and withdrawals, which enhances the overall trading experience. The process is designed to be efficient, allowing for quick fund availability once initiated. Robinhood also provides insights into managing these transfers, ensuring users understand how to maintain liquidity and manage their investments effectively.

Looking ahead, Robinhood continues to innovate and expand its offerings. The platform continually evolves, with new features and tools to enhance user experience and trading capabilities. Upcoming developments may include advanced trading options and improved educational resources to support users' investment decisions. By keeping abreast of these updates, users can maximize their engagement with the app and make informed choices as they navigate the ever-changing investing landscape.

Benefits of Using Robinhood

The benefits of using Robinhood for trading and investing are numerous, making it an appealing option for individuals over 18 looking to open their first trading account. First and foremost, Robinhood offers a user-friendly interface designed specifically for beginners, simplifying buying and selling financial instruments and cryptocurrencies. Whether you are interested in stocks, ETFs, options, or digital currencies, the app provides a seamless experience that allows users to navigate the trading landscape easily. This accessibility empowers new investors to take charge of their financial future without feeling overwhelmed by complex trading platforms.

Another significant benefit of using Robinhood is its commitment to zero-commission trading. This feature allows users to trade without incurring fees typically associated with traditional brokerage firms. By eliminating these costs, Robinhood enables individuals to keep more profits and encourages frequent trading, benefitting those looking to build a diverse portfolio. In addition, the app provides access to fractional shares, allowing users to invest in high-value stocks without needing to purchase a full share, thus lowering the barrier to entry for new investors.

Security is a paramount concern for anyone engaging in online trading, and Robinhood takes this aspect seriously. The app employs robust security features, including two-factor authentication and encryption, to protect user accounts from unauthorized access. Furthermore, Robinhood is a member of the Securities Investor Protection Corporation (SIPC), which provides certain protections for cash and securities held in accounts. These measures contribute to a safer trading environment and instill confidence in users as they navigate their investment journeys.

Regarding financial guarantees, Robinhood also stands out by offering features such as instant deposits, which allow users to access funds immediately after transferring them into their accounts. This capability enhances the trading experience by providing users immediate access to their capital, ensuring they can capitalize on market opportunities without delay. Additionally, the app offers educational resources and trading tools that help users develop effective trading strategies, making it easier to manage risk and make informed decisions.

Lastly, Robinhood is committed to continuous improvement, regularly rolling out new features and updates that enhance the user experience. As the trading landscape evolves, Robinhood adapts by incorporating innovative tools and functionalities that cater to the changing needs of investors. This forward-thinking approach keeps the platform competitive and positions it as a valuable resource for those looking to engage with financial markets modern and efficiently. Whether you are a novice looking to dip your toes into investing or a more experienced trader exploring new opportunities, Robinhood provides a comprehensive suite of benefits designed to support your financial goals.

Chapter 2: Opening Your First Robinhood Account

Setting Up Your Account

Setting up your Robinhood account is a straightforward process designed to be user-friendly for beginners. Download the Robinhood app from your preferred app store or visit the website. Once you have the app, click on the "Sign Up" button, where you will be prompted to provide your email address and create a secure password. After this initial step, you must enter personal information such as your name, date of birth, and Social Security number. This information is crucial for identity verification and compliance with financial regulations.

Security is a top priority for Robinhood, and the platform employs several measures to protect your account. The app uses two-factor authentication (2FA) to add an extra layer of security during the login process. Any sensitive data transmitted through the app is encrypted to prevent unauthorized access. Robinhood also monitors your account for suspicious activity and provides tools for users to manage their privacy settings. This focus on security helps ensure that your trading activities and personal information remain safe.

Once your account is set up and verified, you can begin trading various financial instruments and cryptocurrencies. Robinhood allows users to buy and sell stocks, ETFs, options, and cryptocurrencies—all within a single app. The platform is designed for easy use, featuring a simple interface that guides you through trading. Whether you want to invest in traditional markets or explore the rapidly growing cryptocurrency landscape, Robinhood provides the tools to make informed decisions.

Transferring funds to and from your Robinhood account is also seamless. You must link your account using the Automated Clearing House (ACH) system to fund your account. This process involves verifying your bank account information and may take a few days for the initial transfer. Once linked, you can quickly transfer funds back and forth between your bank and Robinhood, allowing for quick and efficient trading. Understanding how to manage your funds is essential for effective trading and investment strategies.

Looking ahead, Robinhood continues to develop new features and enhancements to improve the user experience. From advanced trading tools to educational resources, the platform aims to empower users with knowledge and capabilities to succeed in their financial journeys. Future developments include expanded access to new asset classes, improved trading analytics, and enhanced security features. Staying informed about these changes will help you make the most of your Robinhood account and adapt to the evolving trading and investing landscape.

Verifying Your Identity

Verifying your identity is a crucial step in opening a Robinhood account. This procedure ensures compliance with federal regulations and protects the platform and its users from fraud. When you create an account, Robinhood will require you to provide personal information such as your name, address, date of birth, and Social Security number. This information helps establish your identity and confirms that you are legally eligible to trade financial instruments and cryptocurrencies on the platform.

To begin the verification process, you must download the Robinhood app and create an account. Once you input your details, the app will prompt you to upload a government-issued identification document, such as a driver's license or passport. Robinhood employs advanced technology to process these documents securely, ensuring your personal information remains protected. This step is essential not only for regulatory compliance but also for safeguarding your account against unauthorized access.

After you submit your identification, Robinhood will conduct a verification check, typically taking only a few minutes. However, in some cases, it may take longer if additional information is required. During this time, the platform assesses whether the information matches its records and whether any discrepancies must be addressed. This thorough verification process is vital to ensuring the safety and security of all users on the platform, as it helps create a trustworthy trading environment.

Once your identity has been verified, you will receive confirmation through the app or email. You can now fund your account and start trading financial instruments or cryptocurrencies. It is essential to understand that verification is not just a one-time step; Robinhood may periodically require re-verification to maintain the integrity of your account and comply with changing regulations. Staying current with these requirements is essential for uninterrupted access to your trading features.

Verifying your identity with Robinhood is a straightforward yet critical component of opening your first account. By following the necessary steps and providing the required information, you contribute to a secure trading environment that protects your funds and personal data. As you embark on your trading journey, keep in mind the importance of maintaining the security of your account and staying informed about any updates or changes in the verification process. This foundational step will set the stage for a successful experience with Robinhood.

Navigating the User Interface

Navigating the user interface of the Robinhood app is an essential skill for any beginner looking to make the most of their investment journey. Upon opening the app, users are greeted with a clean, intuitive layout designed to streamline the trading experience. The main dashboard features an overview of your portfolio, showcasing your investments' performance visually appealingly. This ease of access allows users to monitor their holdings quickly and efficiently, making it easier to make informed decisions about buying or selling financial instruments or cryptocurrencies.

To begin trading, users must familiarize themselves with the bottom navigation bar, which includes links for Home, Search,

Notifications, and Account settings. The Home tab will find market data, trending stocks, and personalized news articles relevant to your investments. The Search functionality lets users explore various financial instruments and cryptocurrencies, providing detailed information on each asset, including historical performance and relevant news. This user-friendly setup is beneficial for beginners, as it simplifies the process of researching potential investments.

Security features are a significant aspect of the Robinhood app, and navigating these settings is vital for ensuring a safe trading experience. Users can access security settings in their Account tab, enabling two-factor authentication, reviewing account activity, and adjusting privacy settings. Understanding these features helps users protect their accounts from unauthorized access and enhances their overall confidence in the platform. Robinhood's commitment to security is crucial, especially for those new to trading, as it reassures users that their financial information and assets are well safeguarded.

Regarding trading, the user interface simplifies the process of executing trades. Users can easily access the trade screen from the asset's page, where they can specify the amount they wish to buy or sell. The app also provides options for setting limit orders, which can help users manage their trades more effectively. The trading interface for those interested in cryptocurrencies remains consistent, allowing for a seamless transition between different asset classes. This uniformity benefits beginners, reducing the learning curve of multiple trading environments.

Lastly, staying updated with new features and developments is crucial for maximizing the Robinhood experience. The app frequently updates, including new trading tools, educational resources, and enhancements to existing features. Users can find information about these developments in the Notifications tab, ensuring they stay informed about the latest opportunities and options available. By actively engaging with the app and exploring its interface, beginners can enhance their trading strategies and maximize their investment journey on Robinhood.

Chapter 3: Security Features of the Robinhood App

Account Protection Measures

Account protection measures are essential for ensuring the security and safety of your investment experience on the Robinhood platform. When opening an account, users should understand the various features and strategies that can help safeguard their financial information and assets. Robinhood employs multiple layers of security, including encryption protocols and two-factor authentication, to protect user accounts from unauthorized access. By taking advantage of these measures, users can help secure their investments and maintain peace of mind while trading.

To further enhance account security, Robinhood encourages users to create strong, unique passwords and change them regularly. A strong password should combine upper- and lowercase letters, numbers, and special characters, making guessing difficult for potential intruders. Additionally, enabling two-factor authentication adds an extra layer of security by requiring a second verification step, usually through a mobile device, when logging into the account. This means that even if someone obtains your password, they still need access to your additional verification method to gain entry.

In addition to user-initiated security measures, Robinhood offers financial guarantees protecting users' investments. The Securities Investor Protection Corporation (SIPC) provides coverage for securities and cash held in customer accounts up to $500,000, which includes a $250,000 limit for cash claims. This safeguard is crucial for users, as it ensures that their investments are protected significantly even in a brokerage failure. Understanding these protections can help users feel more secure in their trading activities.

Transferring funds to and from ACH accounts is another area where security is paramount. Robinhood employs advanced encryption technology to ensure that all transactions are securely processed. Users should verify that their bank information is accurate before initiating transfers and regularly monitor their account statements for suspicious activity. By staying vigilant and informed about their account activity, users can further reduce the risks associated with fund transfers.

As the Robinhood platform evolves, new security features and developments are continually introduced to enhance user protection. Keeping up with these changes is vital for users who want to maximize their account security. Future updates may include improved biometric authentication options or advanced fraud detection systems. By staying informed and proactive, users can ensure they take full advantage of the available protection measures, allowing them to trade financial instruments and cryptocurrencies confidently.

Two-Factor Authentication

Two-factor authentication (2FA) is a crucial security feature that enhances the protection of your Robinhood account. As more individuals engage in online trading, the importance of safeguarding personal financial information cannot be overstated. Two-factor authentication adds an extra layer of security by requiring your password and a second verification form before granting access to your account. This can significantly reduce the risk of unauthorized access, especially in a digital landscape where phishing attacks and data breaches are common.

When you enable 2FA on your Robinhood account, you typically choose between receiving a verification code via SMS or using an authentication app. Each method has its benefits; SMS is straightforward, while authentication apps like Google Authenticator or Authy can provide a more secure option, as they generate time-sensitive codes that cannot be intercepted easily. This dual verification process ensures that even if someone gains access to your password, they still need the second verification form to log in, greatly enhancing your account's security.

Setting up two-factor authentication on Robinhood is a straightforward process. Once you've created your account, navigate to the settings section and look for security options. From there, you can enable 2FA, select your preferred authentication method, and follow the prompts to link your phone number or authentication app. It is essential to complete this setup to fortify your account against potential threats, particularly if you plan to trade financial instruments or cryptocurrencies, which can be lucrative but also attract more cyber threats.

In addition to enabling 2FA, users should remain vigilant about their account security practices. Regularly updating passwords, monitoring account activity, and being cautious of unsolicited communications can further protect against unauthorized access. Robinhood also provides security alerts to notify you of suspicious activity, which can be invaluable for initiating prompt action. By leveraging these security features, you can trade with greater confidence, knowing that your investments and personal information are better protected.

As the trading landscape continues to evolve, Robinhood will likely enhance its security measures further, incorporating more advanced technologies to safeguard user accounts. Staying informed about these developments and actively securing your account through features like two-factor authentication will protect your investments and contribute to a safer trading environment for all users. In a world where digital security is paramount, implementing 2FA is a step every investor should take to secure their financial future.

Understanding Data Encryption

Data encryption is a vital aspect of modern digital security, especially in the context of online trading platforms like Robinhood. It refers to converting information or data into a code to prevent unauthorized access. When you open a Robinhood account, you entrust the platform with sensitive information, including personal identification and financial details. Encryption ensures this data remains confidential and is only accessible to authorized users, such as yourself, and the platform's security systems.

Robinhood employs advanced encryption protocols to protect user data during transmission and storage. For example, when you submit your personal information or execute a trade, that data is encrypted using secure socket layer (SSL) technology. This means that even if a malicious actor intercepts the data packets during transmission, they would only see scrambled information rather than your sensitive details. The robust security measures are crucial for maintaining user trust and ensuring a safe trading environment.

In addition to data in transit, encryption also plays a significant role in the security of stored data. Robinhood encrypts user data at rest, which means that even when your information is stored on their servers, it remains protected. This layer of security prevents unauthorized access to your data, even in the event of a data breach. Robinhood establishes a comprehensive security framework that protects user information against cyber threats by combining encryption in transit and at rest.

Understanding the importance of data encryption is essential for users who want to trade financial instruments and cryptocurrencies. Encrypting your data can give you greater peace of mind, knowing your sensitive information is safeguarded. Furthermore, as you explore the platform's features and functionalities, recognizing how encryption works can help you better appreciate the security measures in place and the importance of maintaining strong personal security practices, such as using unique passwords and enabling two-factor authentication.

As the digital landscape evolves, so does the data encryption technology. Robinhood continuously updates its security protocols to combat emerging threats and ensure compliance with industry standards. Staying informed about these developments is crucial for users, as it enhances their understanding of the platform's security features and empowers them to make informed decisions about their trading activities. Ultimately, understanding data encryption is a key component of navigating the world of online trading safely and effectively.

Chapter 4: Trading Strategies for Financial Instruments on Robinhood

Basics of Stock Trading

Understanding the basics of stock trading is essential for anyone looking to embark on their investment journey, especially with a platform like Robinhood. Stock trading involves buying and selling shares of publicly traded companies. When you buy a stock, you purchase a small ownership stake in that company, and your goal is to sell it later at a higher price than what you paid. The stock market can be volatile, and prices fluctuate based on various factors, including company performance, market conditions, and economic indicators. Educating yourself on these dynamics is crucial to make informed decisions when trading.

Opening an account with the Robinhood app is straightforward and designed for beginners. Users must provide personal information, including their Social Security number, address, and employment details. Once the application is submitted, Robinhood conducts a review, and upon approval, individuals can start trading almost immediately. The app's user-friendly interface simplifies trading for newcomers, allowing them to navigate their portfolios and execute trades quickly. This accessibility has contributed to Robinhood's popularity among first-time investors.

Security is a key concern for anyone engaging in online trading. Robinhood employs security measures to protect user data and funds, including two-factor authentication, encryption protocols, and regular security audits. Additionally, Robinhood is a member of the Securities Investor Protection Corporation (SIPC), which provides limited protection for securities and cash in case of a brokerage failure. Understanding these security features can help users feel more confident in their trading activities.

Trading on Robinhood isn't limited to stocks; users can trade various financial instruments and cryptocurrencies. The app provides access to options trading, ETFs, and digital currencies, making it a versatile platform for diverse investment strategies. However, it's essential to approach these options with caution. Each type of trading has risks and benefits, and new traders should take the time to learn about each market before diving in. A solid trading strategy is essential for managing risk and maximizing potential returns.

Robinhood is at the forefront of integrating new features and improvements as the trading landscape evolves. Recent developments include enhanced research tools, educational resources, and expanded cryptocurrency access. Users should stay informed about these updates, which can significantly impact trading strategies and opportunities. Understanding how to use these features effectively can enhance your trading experience and provide a competitive edge in the market. Engaging with the Robinhood community and utilizing its resources can further bolster your trading journey.

Options Trading Explained

Options trading is a financial strategy allowing investors to speculate on the future price movements of assets without owning the underlying asset. In simple terms, an option is a contract that gives the buyer the right, but not the obligation, to buy or sell an asset at a predetermined price within a specified time frame. This flexibility appeals to novice and experienced traders looking to exploit market volatility. On platforms like Robinhood, options trading has become increasingly accessible, allowing users to engage in this complex financial instrument easily.

When you trade options on Robinhood, you will encounter two primary types: call options and put options. A call option gives the holder the right to purchase an asset at a set price, known as the strike price before the option expires. This strategy is typically employed when an investor anticipates the asset's price will rise. Conversely, a put option allows the holder to sell an asset at the strike price, which is advantageous if the investor expects the asset's price to decline. Understanding these fundamental concepts is essential before diving into options trading.

To participate in options trading on Robinhood, you must enable options trading in your account settings. This process involves agreeing to specific terms and conditions and may require you to provide information regarding your trading experience and financial goals. Once your options trading is enabled, you can explore various strategies, such as covered calls or protective puts. These strategies can help manage risk and potentially enhance returns, making options trading a versatile tool in your investment arsenal.

While options trading can offer substantial rewards, it is not without risks. The potential for loss can be significant, especially for inexperienced traders who may not fully understand the mechanics of options. Consequently, engaging in risk management practices is crucial, such as limiting the amount of capital allocated to options trades and employing stop-loss orders when necessary. Additionally, Robinhood provides educational resources to help users comprehend options trading better and make informed decisions.

As you embark on your options trading journey, stay informed about the evolving landscape of trading platforms like Robinhood. The app consistently introduces new features and enhancements to improve user experience, including advanced charting tools and real-time market data. Embracing these innovations can give you a competitive edge in the fast-paced options trading world, helping you make more intelligent, strategic investment choices.

Creating a Diversified Portfolio

Creating a diversified portfolio is crucial for anyone looking to invest through platforms like Robinhood. A diversified portfolio helps mitigate risk by spreading investments across various asset classes, industries, and geographical regions. You can protect your investment from market volatility by not putting all your eggs in one basket. This strategy is essential for beginners, as it allows you to experience the ups and downs of investing without facing significant losses that can occur from concentrated holdings.

When creating a diversified portfolio on Robinhood, start by considering different asset classes. Stocks, bonds, exchange-traded funds (ETFs), and cryptocurrencies behave differently under various market conditions. For example, bonds may perform better during economic downturns than stocks, while equities can provide higher returns during bullish markets. Robinhood offers a user-friendly interface for purchasing these financial instruments, making it easy for beginners to explore various options and build a balanced portfolio.

Geographic diversification is another crucial aspect to consider. Investing in companies from different countries can reduce the impact of localized economic downturns on your overall portfolio. Robinhood provides access to international stocks and ETFs, allowing you to invest in global markets without the complexities often accompanying foreign investments. This feature particularly appeals to new investors looking to broaden their horizons beyond domestic markets.

Risk tolerance also plays a significant role in portfolio diversification. Assessing your risk appetite will help determine the percentage of your portfolio allocated to higher-risk assets like cryptocurrencies or growth stocks versus more stable options like blue-chip stocks and bonds. Robinhood's platform lets you easily adjust your portfolio as your risk tolerance changes. Additionally, utilizing tools like fractional shares enables you to invest in high-priced stocks without needing a large capital outlay.

Finally, regularly reviewing and rebalancing your portfolio is vital for maintaining diversification. As some investments grow and others decline, the original allocation can shift, increasing risk exposure. Robinhood offers tracking tools to monitor your investments, making it easier to adjust your holdings. Staying informed about market trends and economic indicators will also help guide your decisions, ensuring that your diversified portfolio aligns with your financial goals.

Chapter 5: Cryptocurrency Trading on Robinhood: A Comprehensive Guide

Introduction to Cryptocurrency

Cryptocurrency has emerged as a revolutionary force in the financial landscape, capturing the interest of investors and traders alike. At its core, cryptocurrency is a digital or virtual currency that relies on cryptography for security, making it difficult to counterfeit or double-spend. Unlike traditional currencies governments issue, cryptocurrencies operate on decentralized networks based on blockchain technology. This innovation allows for secure peer-to-peer transactions without intermediaries, such as banks. As you embark on your journey with the Robinhood app, understanding the fundamentals of cryptocurrency will equip you with the knowledge to navigate this digital frontier.

The rise of cryptocurrency has fueled a significant shift in how people perceive and engage with financial markets. With thousands of cryptocurrencies, Bitcoin remains the most recognized and widely adopted. However, other altcoins have gained traction, offering unique features and potential applications. As you explore trading on Robinhood, you must realize the volatility associated with these digital assets. Prices can fluctuate dramatically within short periods, presenting opportunities and risks for traders. Familiarizing yourself with the characteristics of various cryptocurrencies will help you make informed decisions about investing.

Opening a Robinhood account allows you to trade traditional financial instruments and provides access to various cryptocurrencies. The app's user-friendly interface simplifies the trading experience, making it accessible for beginners. Users can easily buy, sell, and hold cryptocurrencies alongside stocks and ETFs, all within a single platform. Robinhood offers commission-free trading, which can be particularly appealing to new investors looking to minimize costs while learning the ropes. This seamless integration of different asset classes enables you to diversify your portfolio effectively.

Safety and security are paramount when dealing with cryptocurrencies, and Robinhood addresses these concerns with various protective measures. The app utilizes advanced encryption technology to safeguard user information and transactions. Additionally, Robinhood is a member of the Securities Investor Protection Corporation (SIPC), which protects securities and cash in case of a brokerage failure. While investing in cryptocurrencies carries inherent risks, understanding the safety features of the Robinhood platform can help mitigate some of these concerns, allowing you to trade with greater confidence.

As the cryptocurrency market continues to evolve, so does the Robinhood app, introducing new features and improvements to enhance user experience. Staying informed about recent developments, such as introducing new cryptocurrencies and updates to trading functionalities, is crucial for maximizing your investment strategy. Moreover, understanding the regulatory landscape surrounding cryptocurrency trading will empower you to navigate potential challenges and opportunities. With the proper knowledge and tools, you can embark on your cryptocurrency trading journey with Robinhood, equipped to make informed decisions in this dynamic marketplace.

Buying and Selling Cryptocurrencies

Buying and selling cryptocurrencies through the Robinhood app is an accessible way for beginners to enter the digital asset market. To get started, users must open a Robinhood account, which involves providing basic personal information and verifying their identity. Once the account is set up, users can fund it through various methods, including linking their bank accounts for ACH transfers. This straightforward process allows users to deposit funds quickly, which is essential for capitalizing on the volatile nature of cryptocurrency prices.

The safety and security of trading on Robinhood are significant concerns for new users. Robinhood employs industry-standard encryption and security measures to protect user data and funds. Two-factor authentication adds a layer of security, ensuring that only authorized users can access their accounts. While no platform can guarantee absolute security, Robinhood has implemented features to mitigate risks associated with trading. Users are encouraged to follow best practices, such as using unique passwords and enabling all available security features to enhance their account protection.

Robinhood offers a user-friendly interface that simplifies the buying and selling process when trading cryptocurrencies. Users can trade cryptocurrencies, including Bitcoin, Ethereum, and Litecoin, with just a few taps on their mobile devices. The app provides real-time market data and charts, enabling users to make informed decisions. However, developing a trading strategy considering market trends and personal risk tolerance is essential, as cryptocurrency markets can be highly volatile.

Understanding the financial guarantees and protections available on Robinhood is crucial for users. While the platform offers commission-free trading, it is essential to note that cryptocurrencies are not covered by the Securities Investor Protection Corporation (SIPC) like traditional securities. However, Robinhood has measures to protect users' funds, including insurance for certain account balances. Users should familiarize themselves with these protections to understand the risks of trading cryptocurrencies on the platform.

As the cryptocurrency market evolves, Robinhood continues to enhance its platform with new features and developments. Future trends include the introduction of more cryptocurrencies, advanced trading tools, and educational resources aimed at helping users navigate the complexities of the digital asset space. Staying informed about these developments can empower users to make more strategic decisions and adapt their trading strategies accordingly. With a solid understanding of how to buy and sell cryptocurrencies on Robinhood, users can confidently participate in this dynamic market.

Understanding Market Trends

Understanding market trends is crucial for anyone navigating the financial landscape successfully, especially using platforms like Robinhood. Market trends refer to the general direction in which the market moves, influenced by various factors such as economic indicators, company performance, and investor sentiment. Recognizing these trends can help investors decide when to enter or exit positions, manage their portfolios, and enhance their trading experiences.

To understand market trends effectively, one must first familiarize themselves with key indicators that signal potential movements. These indicators include price patterns, volume trends, and moving averages. For instance, a rising stock price and increasing trading volume suggest strong investor interest, indicating a bullish trend. Conversely, if prices drop with high volume, this could signal bearish sentiment. Utilizing these indicators on the Robinhood app can provide real-time insights, helping users to capitalize on opportunities as they arise.

Moreover, understanding market trends also involves staying informed about global economic events and news that may impact the financial markets. Economic reports such as employment figures, inflation, and interest rate changes can significantly influence market behavior. Robinhood users should integrate news sources and market analysis into their trading strategies, as timely information can provide a competitive edge. The app's built-in news feed can help users stay updated on relevant developments that could affect their investments.

Another critical aspect of understanding market trends is recognizing the role of sentiment analysis. Market sentiment reflects the overall attitude of investors towards a particular security or market. Tools like social media sentiment trackers or trading volume analysis can provide insights into other investors' feelings about specific stocks or cryptocurrencies. By gauging this sentiment, Robinhood users can better position themselves in the market, aligning their strategies with prevailing trends.

Lastly, understanding market trends becomes even more vital as the investing landscape evolves, especially with the rise of new financial instruments and cryptocurrencies. Robinhood consistently updates its platform to include new features and tools that help users analyze trends more effectively. Keeping abreast of such developments enhances trading strategies and reinforces users' confidence in investment decisions. By combining knowledge of market trends with the user-friendly tools offered by Robinhood, beginners can embark on their investing journey with greater assurance and potential for success.

Chapter 6: Understanding Financial Guarantees and Protections on Robinhood

Insurance for Your Investments

When you begin your investment journey with the Robinhood app, understanding the insurance available for your investments is crucial. Robinhood is a Securities Investor Protection Corporation (SIPC) member, which protects customers if the brokerage firm fails. SIPC insurance covers up to $500,000 in securities and cash, with a limit of $250,000 for money alone. While this does not protect against market losses, it provides a layer of protection against the potential insolvency of the brokerage firm, giving investors peace of mind as they navigate the trading landscape.

In addition to SIPC protection, Robinhood takes further steps to ensure the safety of your assets. The app implements robust security measures, including two-factor authentication and encryption, to help safeguard your account from unauthorized access. These features work with SIPC coverage to create a secure trading environment. Investors must adopt best practices to enhance their security alongside institutional protections, such as using strong passwords and regularly monitoring account activity.

When trading financial instruments and cryptocurrencies, it is vital to understand that while SIPC provides insurance for your assets, it does not extend to the assets themselves in the event of market downturns. Investors should know the inherent risks associated with trading, especially in the volatile cryptocurrency market. This awareness fosters better risk management and encourages investors to diversify their portfolios, which can mitigate potential losses during unfavorable market conditions.

Transferring funds to and from your ACH accounts is another aspect of managing your investments that requires attention. Robinhood facilitates easy transfers, but monitoring these transactions closely is vital to ensure accuracy and security. Although the app provides a seamless experience, discrepancies could affect your trading capabilities. Being vigilant about your fund transfers will help you control your investment activities and ensure that your capital is always readily available for trading opportunities.

As Robinhood continues to innovate and introduce new features, staying informed about these developments is essential for maximizing your investment strategy. The platform regularly updates its offerings, which may include enhanced security features or new financial products. By remaining engaged with the latest trends and updates, you can take full advantage of what Robinhood offers while ensuring that your investments are protected through insurance and security measures. As a new investor, understanding these elements can help you build a solid foundation for a successful investment journey.

SIPC Protection Explained

SIPC protection, or Securities Investor Protection Corporation protection, is a crucial aspect of investing that every Robinhood user should understand. SIPC was created to protect customers if a brokerage firm fails. While SIPC does not protect against losses from the decline in value of investments, it provides a safety net for the securities and cash held in your brokerage account up to certain limits. Specifically, it covers up to $500,000 per customer, which includes a limit of $250,000 for cash claims. If Robinhood were to go out of business, the SIPC would help recover your assets within these limits.

Understanding the nuances of SIPC protection can provide peace of mind when trading through the Robinhood app. It's important to note that SIPC coverage applies only to brokerage accounts. Therefore, those assets do not fall under SIPC protection if you trade cryptocurrencies on Robinhood. As a beginner, ensuring that your investments in stocks and ETFs are safeguarded under SIPC can help you feel more secure as you navigate the trading landscape. Learning about these protections is essential to making informed decisions regarding your investments.

In addition to SIPC protection, Robinhood employs various security features to protect users' accounts and personal information. The platform utilizes two-factor authentication, encryption, and other security measures to safeguard sensitive data. This means that even if a hacker gains access to your login credentials, additional verification steps are in place to prevent unauthorized access. By familiarizing yourself with these security protocols, you can enhance your overall safety while using the app, making it a more secure environment for trading financial instruments and cryptocurrencies.

When transferring funds to and from your Robinhood account using ACH (Automated Clearing House), understanding the mechanics of these transactions is vital. ACH transfers offer a seamless way to deposit or withdraw funds, but typically take several business days to process. It is essential to plan your trades accordingly, especially if you expect to access your funds quickly. Knowing that SIPC protection applies to your securities can also alleviate concerns about these transactions, as you can feel confident that your investments are secure during the transfer process.

As Robinhood continues to evolve, staying informed about new developments and features is essential for maximizing your trading experience. The platform frequently updates its offerings to enhance user experience and security. Awareness of these changes can give you additional tools and resources to manage your investments effectively. By understanding SIPC protection and other safety features, you can confidently approach your trading journey, knowing that your financial interests are safeguarded as you explore the investing world.

Risk Disclosure and User Responsibility

Risk disclosure is essential to engaging with any financial platform, including Robinhood. As users embark on their journey of trading financial instruments and cryptocurrencies, it is crucial to understand that all forms of investing carry inherent risks. Investment performance can fluctuate, and while the profit potential exists, there is also the possibility of incurring losses. Robinhood provides various resources to help users comprehend these risks. Still, it remains the responsibility of each user to fully understand the implications of their trading decisions and conduct their research.

Robinhood has implemented several security features to safeguard user accounts and personal information. These include two-factor authentication, encryption of sensitive data, and regular security assessments. Despite these measures, no platform is entirely immune to risks such as hacking or fraud. Users must be vigilant about their account security, including choosing strong passwords and being cautious of phishing attempts. Understanding the security framework of the Robinhood app can empower users to take proactive steps to protect their assets.

Users can trade financial instruments on Robinhood, including stocks, ETFs, options, and cryptocurrencies. Each market has its risk profile, and users should familiarize themselves with the specific factors that can influence the performance of their investments. Additionally, Robinhood offers educational resources and tutorials that can aid in developing effective trading strategies. Beginners should start small, gaining experience and confidence before committing more significant amounts of capital.

Financial guarantees and protections are also pivotal for users of the Robinhood platform. Robinhood is a member of the Securities Investor Protection Corporation (SIPC), which provides limited protection for securities and cash in case of broker failure. However, this protection does not cover losses due to market fluctuations. Users should know this distinction and consider how it impacts their investment strategies. Understanding these financial guarantees can provide comfort but should not replace diligent risk management practices.

Finally, as Robinhood continues to innovate and introduce new features, keeping abreast of these developments can enhance the trading experience. The platform regularly updates its offerings, which may include improved trading tools, educational resources, or new asset classes. Users are encouraged to stay informed about these changes and to adapt their trading strategies accordingly. Ultimately, while Robinhood provides a user-friendly interface and a wealth of resources, the onus of responsible trading and risk management lies with the individual, making it essential to approach investing with caution and due diligence.

Chapter 7: Step-by-Step Guide to Transferring Funds to and from ACH Accounts

Linking Your Bank Account

Linking your bank account to your Robinhood account is a crucial step enabling you to trade financial instruments and cryptocurrencies seamlessly. To begin the process, you must navigate to the account settings within the Robinhood app. Here, you will find the option to link a bank account. The app typically provides a straightforward interface where you can choose your bank from a list or manually enter your bank account details. This functionality is essential because it allows for quick deposits and withdrawals, making your trading experience efficient.

Once you select your bank, you will be prompted to enter your login credentials for your online banking account. This process utilizes secure encryption methods, ensuring your sensitive information is protected. Robinhood employs bank-level security features, which include two-factor authentication and data encryption, to safeguard your financial information. These measures help to reassure users that their accounts remain secure while facilitating easy transfers to and from their Robinhood accounts.

After linking your bank account, you can initiate transfers via the Automated Clearing House (ACH) network. This process is generally quick, allowing deposits to be available for trading within a few days. It's important to note that while transfers may take some time to process, Robinhood offers a feature called "Instant Deposits," which allows you to access a portion of your funds immediately. However, be aware that there are limits on how much you can withdraw until your deposits are apparent, and understanding these limits is crucial for effective trading.

In addition to the safety measures, Robinhood also adheres to financial guarantees to protect users. The Securities Investor Protection Corporation (SIPC) insures your securities up to $500,000, which includes a $250,000 limit for cash claims. This insurance offers an added layer of security, ensuring that your assets remain protected even in the unlikely event of a brokerage failure. By understanding these financial protections, users can trade more confidently, knowing their investments are secure.

As the Robinhood platform continues to evolve, new features and developments are regularly introduced to enhance user experience. Recent updates have focused on improving security protocols and expanding the range of financial instruments available for trading. Stay informed about these changes, as they can significantly impact your trading strategies and overall experience. By linking your bank account effectively and understanding the associated security measures, you can embark on your trading journey with greater assurance and knowledge.

Making Deposits

Making deposits in your Robinhood account is a crucial step in your journey towards trading financial instruments and cryptocurrencies. The next logical step after successfully opening your account is funding it to buy stocks, ETFs, and cryptocurrencies. Robinhood offers several options for making deposits, primarily through bank transfers. To initiate a deposit, you must link your bank account to your Robinhood account using the Automated Clearing House (ACH) system. This straightforward process lets you enter your bank details directly in the app. Once linked, you can quickly transfer funds whenever necessary.

When you make a deposit, it typically takes a few business days for the funds to clear and become available for trading. However, Robinhood provides a feature called Instant Deposits, which allows you to access a portion of your deposit immediately, up to a specific limit. This feature mainly benefits traders who want to seize market opportunities without waiting for the full deposit to process. It is important to note that instant access applies only to deposits within your established limits, which are determined by various factors, including your account history and trading activity.

Security is a primary concern for anyone dealing with financial transactions, and Robinhood takes this aspect seriously. The platform employs various security measures to protect your personal and financial information. This includes encryption protocols and two-factor authentication, which adds an extra layer of security to your account. Furthermore, Robinhood is a member of the Financial Industry Regulatory Authority (FINRA) and the Securities Investor Protection Corporation (SIPC), providing additional assurance that your funds are safeguarded up to a specified limit in case of financial mishaps.

Transferring funds to and from your Robinhood account is facilitated through the ACH network, a secure and widely used method for electronic payments. When you wish to withdraw funds, the process is similar to making a deposit. You initiate a transfer request through the app, and the funds will be sent back to your linked bank account. While deposits are generally processed quickly, withdrawals may take longer, typically between three to five business days, depending on your bank's processing times.

As Robinhood continues to evolve, new features and developments are regularly introduced to enhance the user experience. Future updates may include improved deposit and withdrawal options, additional cryptocurrencies for trading, and advanced trading tools for more experienced investors. Keeping an eye on these developments can help you take full advantage of what Robinhood offers. For those just starting, understanding the process of making deposits and the associated security measures is essential for building a solid foundation in trading.

Withdrawing Funds

Withdrawing funds from your Robinhood account is a straightforward process designed to give users easy access to their money. After successfully trading financial instruments or cryptocurrencies, you can transfer your earnings back to your linked bank account. To initiate a withdrawal, navigate to the "Account" tab within the app, select "Transfers," and choose "Withdraw to Your Bank." From there, you can specify the amount you wish to withdraw. It is essential to ensure that your bank account is correctly linked to your Robinhood account to facilitate smooth transactions.

The time it takes for funds to be withdrawn can vary, but typically, Robinhood processes withdrawal requests within 2 to 3 business days. However, the actual time for the funds to appear in your bank account may depend on your bank's processing times. Users should keep in mind that, in some cases, funds from recent trades may not be immediately available for withdrawal due to the settlement period of the securities. If you sell a stock, the proceeds might not be accessible for withdrawal until the transaction has fully settled, which usually takes two business days.

Security is a primary concern for all financial transactions, and Robinhood has implemented several measures to ensure that your funds are safe. The platform uses bank-level encryption to protect your data and employs two-factor authentication to add a layer of security to your account. Furthermore, if you have any concerns about unauthorized transactions, Robinhood offers prompt customer support to address any issues. It is advisable to regularly monitor your account activity to ensure that all transactions are legitimate.

In addition to security measures, it is wise to familiarize yourself with Robinhood's financial guarantees. As a member of the Financial Industry Regulatory Authority (FINRA) and the Securities Investor Protection Corporation (SIPC), Robinhood provides specific protections for your funds and securities. SIPC coverage protects customers up to $500,000, including up to $250,000 for cash claims, if a brokerage firm goes bankrupt or experiences financial difficulties. Understanding these protections can give you peace of mind while trading.

As Robinhood continues to evolve, new features and developments are frequently introduced to enhance user experience. These updates may include improvements in the withdrawal process, adding new financial instruments available for trading, or more robust security features. Staying informed about these developments is crucial for maximizing your trading experience. Keep an eye on Robinhood's announcements and updates to ensure you utilize all the available tools and features to manage your investments effectively.

Chapter 8: Exploring New Features and Developments in the Robinhood App

Recent Updates and Enhancements

Recent updates and enhancements to the Robinhood app have significantly improved the user experience and expanded its functionality for novice and experienced traders. One of the most notable advancements is the introduction of advanced charting tools and in-depth analytical features that allow users to make more informed trading decisions. These tools provide real-time data, customizable indicators, and historical performance metrics, making analyzing trends and executing trades easier. This enhancement aligns with the growing demand for more sophisticated trading capabilities among users who want to engage with financial markets strategically.

In addition to analytical tools, Robinhood has also made strides in enhancing its security features. Recent updates include two-factor authentication improvements and enhanced encryption protocols to safeguard user data and account information. Security remains a primary concern for online traders, so these enhancements are crucial in building user trust and protecting sensitive information against potential breaches. Robinhood's commitment to maintaining a secure trading environment is evident in its continuous efforts to update its security measures in line with industry standards.

The trading experience on Robinhood has also evolved with the introduction of new financial instruments and expanded cryptocurrency options. Users can now trade various stocks,

ETFs, and a growing list of cryptocurrencies, including popular options such as Bitcoin and Ethereum. This expansion allows users to diversify their portfolios more efficiently and explore new investment opportunities. Furthermore, Robinhood has introduced educational resources within the app, offering users insights into trading strategies and market trends, which is particularly beneficial for beginners.

Transferring funds to and from ACH accounts has also seen improvements in the Robinhood app, with a streamlined process that enables quicker transactions. Users can now initiate transfers more quickly, making it convenient to deposit funds for trading or withdraw profits. The updates to the fund transfer process include more explicit guidelines and enhanced tracking features, allowing users to monitor their transactions in real-time; this is a significant improvement for users who require quick access to their funds for trading or personal expenses.

Looking ahead, Robinhood continues to innovate with plans for future developments to enhance user experience even further. Features such as fractional trading, automatic rebalancing, and expanded research tools are on the horizon, catering to the evolving needs of the trading community. As the financial landscape shifts, Robinhood's commitment to adapting and improving its platform will likely keep it at the forefront of online trading, making it an appealing choice for those looking to navigate the complexities of investing in today's markets.

Future Plans for the Platform

As Robinhood continues evolving, the platform aims to enhance user experience and expand trading opportunities. One significant focus is on improving the educational resources available to users. The platform recognizes that many individuals are new to investing and trading, and as such, it is committed to providing comprehensive guides, tutorials, and market analysis. These resources will cover the basics of opening a Robinhood account and delve deeper into advanced trading and risk management techniques. Robinhood aims to foster a more informed trading community by empowering users with knowledge.

Another key area of development is the expansion of trading options. Robinhood has already made strides in offering a variety of financial instruments, including stocks, ETFs, options, and cryptocurrencies. Plans include the introduction of new asset classes and the possibility of allowing users to trade fractional shares of more securities. This will enable investors of all sizes to diversify their portfolios and make investments that align with their financial goals. Additionally, Robinhood is exploring partnerships with other financial institutions to facilitate access to international markets, further broadening its trading capabilities.

Security remains a top priority for Robinhood as it plans for the future. With the increasing prevalence of cyber threats, the platform invests in advanced security measures to protect user data and transactions. Future updates may include enhanced two-factor authentication methods, real-time fraud detection systems, and improved encryption protocols. Ensuring that users feel secure while trading is crucial for Robinhood, primarily as it seeks to attract a broader demographic of investors who may be apprehensive about the safety of online trading.

Robinhood is also committed to enhancing the user interface and overall user experience. Upcoming updates may feature a more intuitive app design, making it easier for users to navigate through various functionalities. This includes streamlining the process of transferring funds to and from ACH accounts, which is critical for many investors. By simplifying these processes, Robinhood aims to reduce barriers for new users and create a more seamless trading experience for all.

Lastly, Robinhood continuously monitors trends in the financial markets and user feedback to shape its future direction. The platform is keen on integrating cutting-edge technology, such as artificial intelligence and machine learning, to offer personalized trading insights and recommendations. As trading and investing evolve, Robinhood's adaptability will be essential in meeting its users' demands. By focusing on education, security, user experience, and innovative technology, Robinhood is well-positioned to lead the way in democratizing finance for everyone over 18 years of age.

User Feedback and Development

User feedback plays a crucial role in the continuous development of the Robinhood app, shaping the features and functionalities that users engage with daily. As a platform that caters to a diverse audience over 18 years of age, Robinhood values the insights provided by its users. Feedback on ease of account creation, security measures, and trading functionalities informs the company's decisions on enhancements and new developments. By actively soliciting user input, Robinhood improves the user experience and builds a community that feels invested in the platform's evolution.

The safety and security features of the Robinhood app are often a focal point for user feedback. Users frequently express concerns about protecting personal information and the integrity of their financial transactions. In response, Robinhood has implemented advanced security measures, including two-factor authentication and encryption protocols, which are frequently updated based on user suggestions and emerging security threats. This ongoing dialogue between users and the development team ensures that the app remains a secure environment for trading financial instruments and cryptocurrencies.

Regarding trading strategies, user feedback provides invaluable insights into the features that most benefit novice and experienced traders. Suggestions regarding educational resources, trading tools, and analytics have led to introducing features that assist users in making informed decisions. By understanding the needs of its user base, Robinhood can refine its trading platform, making it easier for users to navigate the complexities of financial markets and implement effective trading strategies.

Another area where user feedback has driven development is transferring funds to and from ACH accounts. Many users have shared their experiences regarding the speed and efficiency of fund transfers, prompting Robinhood to optimize this process. By addressing these concerns, Robinhood ensures that users can quickly and easily access their funds, facilitating seamless trading experiences. Clear communication about financial guarantees and protections also helps users feel more secure when managing their investments.

Looking toward the future, Robinhood continues to explore new features and developments based on user feedback. The company remains committed to staying ahead of trends in trading and investing, leveraging user insights to prioritize enhancements that align with evolving market needs. This proactive approach strengthens the platform and fosters a sense of community among users, who play an integral role in shaping the future of Robinhood. As the platform evolves, ongoing user feedback will remain a cornerstone of its development strategy, ensuring it meets the demands of an ever-changing financial landscape.

Chapter 9: Risk Management and Safety Tips for Robinhood Users

Setting Realistic Expectations

Setting realistic expectations is crucial when embarking on your journey with the Robinhood app. Many new users may envision instant wealth or seamless trading experiences without fully understanding the complexities involved in investing. It is essential to recognize that while Robinhood offers user-friendly access to financial markets, success in trading requires patience, knowledge, and a clear understanding of personal financial goals. Setting achievable expectations allows you to navigate the platform more effectively and avoid common pitfalls that lead to frustration or disappointment.

When opening a Robinhood account, it's essential to understand that trading financial instruments and cryptocurrencies involves inherent risks. Prices can fluctuate dramatically, and the potential for loss is real. While the app provides tools and resources to help you make informed decisions, new traders should not expect to become experts overnight. Instead, approach your trading journey as a learning experience. Start with small investments, familiarize yourself with the market dynamics, and gradually build your confidence and expertise.

Security is another vital aspect to consider when using Robinhood. The app employs various security features to protect users' accounts and personal information, but no system is entirely immune to risks. Understanding these security measures can help you feel more secure as you trade. However, setting realistic expectations regarding your responsibility to maintain account security is essential, such as using strong passwords and enabling two-factor authentication. A proactive approach to security can significantly reduce the likelihood of unauthorized access to your account.

Financial guarantees and protections are also crucial in shaping your expectations. Robinhood provides specific protections for users, such as SIPC insurance, which covers a portion of your cash and securities in case of a broker failure. However, this does not safeguard against market losses. Users should be aware that while Robinhood offers a platform for trading, the responsibility for managing investments and understanding the risks involved ultimately lies with them. Recognizing this reality can foster a more balanced perspective on the potential outcomes of trading.

Finally, as you engage with Robinhood, keep an eye on new developments and features the platform introduces. The financial landscape constantly evolves, and Robinhood will likely adapt and enhance its offerings. Setting realistic expectations means being open to learning and adjusting your strategies based on market conditions and technological advancements. By staying informed and adaptable, you can position yourself to take advantage of new opportunities while minimizing risks and enhancing your overall trading experience.

Understanding Market Volatility

Market volatility refers to the degree of variation in the price of financial instruments over a given period. It is an inherent aspect of trading and investing, reflecting the rapid changes that can occur in response to economic indicators, corporate earnings, geopolitical events, and changes in investor sentiment.

Understanding market volatility is crucial for beginners using platforms like Robinhood as it can significantly impact trading decisions, investment strategies, and overall portfolio performance. Recognizing when markets are likely volatile can help traders manage risk more effectively and make informed investment choices.

Volatility can be measured in several ways, with one common method being calculating the standard deviation of returns over a specific timeframe. A higher standard deviation indicates greater volatility, meaning prices are likely to fluctuate more widely. This concept is essential for users of Robinhood, particularly those interested in trading stocks, options, and cryptocurrencies. By understanding how volatility affects different asset classes, traders can better anticipate market movements and adjust their strategies accordingly. For instance, cryptocurrencies are often more volatile than traditional stocks, leading to higher potential returns and increased risk.

Investors often employ various strategies to navigate market volatility, including diversification, hedging, and utilizing stop-loss orders. Diversification involves spreading investments across different asset classes to reduce exposure to any market segment. Hedging, conversely, consists of taking positions in financial instruments expected to move inversely to existing investments, thereby mitigating potential losses. For Robinhood users, these strategies can be easily implemented through the app's user-friendly interface, enabling even novice investors to manage their portfolios effectively in turbulent market conditions.

Moreover, understanding the implications of market volatility is not just about managing risk; it can also present opportunities. Heightened volatility often creates pricing inefficiencies, allowing savvy traders to capitalize on temporary discrepancies in asset valuations. For those new to trading on Robinhood, this means that even in a fluctuating market, there are chances to buy low and sell high, provided that traders remain informed and disciplined in their approach. Utilizing market research tools and staying updated on current events can enhance decision-making during these periods of uncertainty.

Finally, as markets continue to evolve, new developments in trading technology and platforms like Robinhood are making it easier for users to navigate volatility. Features like real-time market data, advanced charting tools, and educational resources are becoming increasingly accessible. By leveraging these tools, beginners can better understand market dynamics and refine their trading strategies, ultimately leading to a more confident and informed trading experience. As you embark on your journey with Robinhood, embracing the complexities of market volatility will be essential to cultivating a successful investment approach.

Developing a Risk Management Plan

Developing a risk management plan is crucial for anyone venturing into the trading world, especially when using platforms like the Robinhood app. This plan should encompass various strategies to identify, assess, and mitigate potential risks associated with trading financial instruments and cryptocurrencies. As an investor, understanding the inherent risks of the markets you are entering is essential to safeguard your investments and ensure a more secure trading experience.

The first component of a risk management plan is to set clear investment goals. Identify both short-term and long-term objectives and the level of risk you are willing to tolerate for each investment. This clarity will help guide your trading decisions and influence the types of financial instruments you choose to engage with on Robinhood. Defining goals will help you maintain a disciplined approach even amid market volatility, whether focused on growth stocks, dividend-paying equities, or cryptocurrencies.

Next, diversifying your portfolio is a fundamental principle in risk management. By spreading your investments across various asset classes, you reduce the impact of a poor-performing investment on your overall portfolio. Robinhood allows users to easily invest in multiple financial instruments, from stocks to ETFs and even cryptocurrencies. This flexibility enables you to create a diversified portfolio that can better withstand market fluctuations while aligning with your risk tolerance and investment goals.

Monitoring your investments is another critical aspect of your risk management plan. Regularly reviewing your portfolio and tracking market trends can help you make informed decisions about when to buy or sell assets. Robinhood provides tools and resources for tracking your investments, including price alerts and real-time market data, which can aid you in making timely adjustments. Staying informed about the latest developments in financial markets and the specific assets you are invested in will empower you to mitigate risks effectively.

Lastly, it is essential to establish exit strategies and risk limits. Define the conditions under which you would sell an asset, whether due to reaching a specific price point or a change in market conditions. Setting stop-loss orders can further protect your investments by automatically selling assets when they get a predetermined price. Utilizing these strategies helps minimize losses and enhances your overall trading discipline in a platform like Robinhood, where trading is easily accessible; having a solid risk management plan can significantly improve your trading experience and contribute to long-term success.

Chapter 10: Comparing Robinhood with Other Trading Platforms in Terms of Security

Overview of Competitor Platforms

Robinhood has carved a niche in online trading and investing by offering a user-friendly platform catering to newcomers and experienced investors. However, it's essential to understand how Robinhood stacks up against its competitors. Platforms such as E*TRADE, TD Ameritrade, and Fidelity offer robust trading environments with their unique features, advantages, and drawbacks. A comparative overview of these competitor platforms can provide valuable insights for potential users considering where to open their accounts.

E*TRADE is well-known for its comprehensive trading tools and educational resources, making it an attractive option for those seeking a more hands-on approach to investing. With advanced charting capabilities and a wide variety of investment vehicles, including stocks, ETFs, options, and mutual funds, E*TRADE appeals to active traders. However, unlike Robinhood, which offers commission-free trades, E*TRADE charges fees for certain transactions, which could deter beginner investors just starting to build their portfolios.

TD Ameritrade stands out with its extensive research offerings and educational content, providing users with a wealth of information to make informed investment decisions. The platform also features advanced trading platforms like Thinkorswim, designed for serious traders requiring sophisticated analysis tools. While TD Ameritrade provides robust security features, including two-factor authentication and encryption, its fee structure can be a drawback for those looking for a free trading experience similar to Robinhood offers.

Fidelity is recognized for its exceptional customer service and investor education resources. It provides a range of investment options, including zero-fee index funds, which appeal to long-term investors. Fidelity also offers a user-friendly mobile app, making it easier for users to manage their investments. However, like E*TRADE and TD Ameritrade, Fidelity charges for specific trades and services, which may not be as appealing to the cost-conscious beginner investor looking for a no-fee platform like Robinhood.

When considering which platform to choose, evaluating the fee structures, security features, ease of use, and available resources is crucial. Robinhood's streamlined interface and commission-free trading attract many new investors, but it is vital to weigh these benefits against the offerings of established competitors. Understanding the strengths and weaknesses of platforms like E*TRADE, TD Ameritrade, and Fidelity can help investors make informed decisions that align with their financial goals and investing strategies.

Security Features Comparison

Security features are paramount when considering a trading platform, especially for those new to investing. Robinhood has implemented various security measures to protect users' accounts and personal information. One of the most prominent features is two-factor authentication (2FA), which adds an extra layer of security beyond the standard username and password. Users are encouraged to enable this feature, as it requires a second form of verification, typically through a mobile device, whenever there's a sign-in attempt from an unrecognized device.

Robinhood's security protocols are competitive but vary in certain areas compared to other trading platforms. While many platforms offer similar 2FA options, Robinhood stands out with its robust encryption technology. All data transmitted between users and the app is encrypted, ensuring that sensitive information remains secure. Additionally, Robinhood monitors accounts for unauthorized activity, alerting users about potential security breaches, a critical feature in today's digital landscape.

Financial guarantees also play a significant role in assessing the security of a trading platform. Robinhood is a member of the Financial Industry Regulatory Authority (FINRA) and the Securities Investor Protection Corporation (SIPC). This membership provides users with coverage for securities and cash in the event of brokerage failure, up to $500,000, including a maximum of $250,000 for cash claims. This protection offers a level of reassurance for users, especially those new to the investment world who may be concerned about the safety of their funds.

Robinhood utilizes Automated Clearing House (ACH) transfers, generally secure and efficient when transferring funds. Users can link their bank accounts to facilitate funds transfers to and from their Robinhood account. While these transfers are typically processed within a few days, Robinhood employs bank-grade security measures to protect users' financial information during these transactions, making it a reliable option for managing funds.

As technology evolves, so do the security features on trading platforms like Robinhood. The company continually updates its system to counter emerging threats and improve user safety. Future developments may include advanced biometric authentication, AI-driven fraud detection, and enhanced data privacy measures. Staying informed about these updates is crucial for users, as they can significantly impact the overall security of their trading experience.

Pros and Cons of Each Platform

The various trading platforms available have advantages and disadvantages that can significantly affect a user's experience. Robinhood, known for its user-friendly interface and commission-free trading, stands out in the market. One of its primary advantages is accessibility. The app is designed for beginners, allowing users to quickly open an account and start trading without the complexities often associated with traditional brokerages. This simplicity can appeal to those unfamiliar with investing, making navigating financial instruments and cryptocurrencies easier.

However, the ease of use does not come without drawbacks. One notable concern is the limited research and educational resources provided by Robinhood. While the platform is intuitive, the lack of in-depth analysis tools may hinder more experienced traders from seeking comprehensive information to inform their decisions. This gap can disadvantage individuals looking to implement sophisticated trading strategies or conduct detailed market research. As a result, users may need to rely on external resources to supplement their trading knowledge, which can be inconvenient.

In terms of security, Robinhood employs various measures to protect user data and funds, including two-factor authentication and encryption. These features contribute to a generally safe trading environment, which is essential for users concerned about the safety of their investments. However, past incidents, such as outages during peak trading times and security breaches, have raised questions about the platform's reliability. While the company has made strides in addressing these issues, potential users should remain vigilant and consider the overall security posture of the platform before committing their funds.

Financial guarantees on Robinhood also play a crucial role in its appeal. The platform is a member of the Securities Investor Protection Corporation (SIPC), which protects customers against the loss of cash and securities in case of a brokerage failure up to a specific limit. This safety net can provide some peace of mind for new investors, knowing that their investments are somewhat safeguarded. Nevertheless, users should understand that SIPC does not protect against losses due to market fluctuations, posing inherent trading risks.

Finally, when comparing Robinhood with other trading platforms, it's essential to consider the evolving landscape of investing technology. While Robinhood has pioneered several new developments, such as cryptocurrency trading and innovative features to enhance user experience, other platforms may offer more robust tools and analytics for serious traders. This ongoing competition could lead to exciting advancements in trading capabilities. Still, users should weigh the pros and cons of each platform carefully, ensuring they choose one that aligns with their trading style and financial goals.

Chapter 11: Future Trends in Trading and Investing with Robinhood

The Rise of Retail Investors

The rise of retail investors has fundamentally transformed the landscape of financial markets, empowering individuals to take control of their investment journeys. Traditionally, investing was the domain of institutional investors and high-net-worth individuals. However, the advent of technology and user-friendly platforms like Robinhood has democratized access to financial markets, enabling everyday people to engage in trading and investing. The proliferation of smartphones, social media, and an increasing desire for economic independence among younger generations has fueled this shift.

Robinhood, in particular, has emerged as a key player in this transformation by offering commission-free trading and a streamlined interface that appeals to novice and experienced investors. The platform's accessibility has encouraged millions to open accounts and explore various financial instruments, from stocks to options and cryptocurrencies. As retail investors gain confidence and knowledge, they influence market trends and behavior, often leveraging social media to share insights and strategies. This newfound community aspect has fostered a sense of belonging among investors previously isolated in their financial endeavors.

Security is a paramount concern for anyone venturing into online trading, and Robinhood has implemented several features to ensure the safety of its users. The platform employs advanced encryption and security protocols to protect personal and financial information. Additionally, Robinhood is a member of the Financial Industry Regulatory Authority (FINRA) and the Securities Investor Protection Corporation (SIPC), which provides certain protections for investors. Understanding these security measures is crucial for new users navigating the platform and engaging in trading activities.

Regarding trading strategies, retail investors on Robinhood have access to various financial instruments and the ability to trade cryptocurrencies. The platform's educational resources and user-friendly design provide a solid foundation for developing trading strategies. Whether opting for long-term investments or short-term trading, users can explore different approaches tailored to their financial goals. Furthermore, Robinhood's recent expansions into cryptocurrency trading have attracted new investors eager to capitalize on the volatile but potentially lucrative digital asset market.

As Robinhood continues to evolve, new features and developments are on the horizon, further enhancing the trading experience. The platform will likely introduce additional educational tools, advanced trading options, and improved risk management resources. Retail investors are encouraged to stay informed about these updates, which can significantly impact trading strategies and overall market participation. By understanding the current landscape and being aware of future trends, users can position themselves to maximize their investment opportunities while navigating the dynamic world of retail trading.

Innovations in Trading Technology

Trading technology innovations have transformed how individuals engage with financial markets, making them more accessible and user-friendly. Robinhood, a pioneer in this space, has leveraged technological advancements to create a platform that caters to beginner investors. The app's design facilitates a seamless experience, allowing users to open an account quickly and start trading with minimal barriers. These innovations not only streamline the process of account creation but also enhance the overall user experience, encouraging more people to participate in investing.

One of the key innovations in trading technology is the introduction of commission-free trading. Robinhood's model eliminates traditional brokerage fees, which can often deter new investors from entering the market. This approach democratizes trading, enabling users to invest in financial instruments and cryptocurrencies without worrying about transaction costs. Moreover, the app's intuitive interface and educational resources empower beginners to make informed decisions, fostering a culture of self-directed investing that was less accessible in previous generations.

Security is paramount in the digital trading landscape, and Robinhood has implemented several cutting-edge features to protect user data and financial assets. The app employs bank-level encryption and two-factor authentication to safeguard accounts against unauthorized access. Additionally, Robinhood is a member of the Securities Investor Protection Corporation (SIPC), which provides limited protection for securities and cash in case of brokerage failure. These measures instill confidence in users, assuring them that their investments are secure while they explore the platform's capabilities.

As the trading landscape evolves, Robinhood remains at the forefront of integrating new features and technology. Recent developments include the introduction of cryptocurrency trading, enhancing the app's appeal to a broader audience. Users can now buy, sell, and hold various cryptocurrencies, reflecting a growing trend towards digital assets. Additionally, Robinhood is continually refining its platform based on user feedback, ensuring that it meets the needs of its community while staying ahead of competitors in the market.

Looking to the future, the innovations in trading technology promise to facilitate even more significant advancements in how individuals engage with their investments. The potential for features such as artificial intelligence-driven trading recommendations, enhanced risk management tools, and further integrations with financial education platforms could revolutionize the trading experience. As Robinhood and similar platforms evolve, they will likely continue to empower individuals to take control of their financial futures in an increasingly dynamic market environment.

The Evolving Landscape of Financial Apps

The financial technology landscape has significantly transformed in recent years, reflecting the rapid evolution of consumer needs and technological advancements. Financial apps, particularly trading platforms like Robinhood, have democratized access to investing, allowing individuals from diverse backgrounds to participate in the stock and cryptocurrency markets. This shift has made it easier for beginners over 18 to open and manage investment accounts, as the barriers to entry have lowered remarkably. The Robinhood app, known for its user-friendly interface and commission-free trading, exemplifies this trend, attracting a new generation of investors who seek simplicity and efficiency in their trading experience.

Safety and security are paramount in financial apps, and Robinhood is no exception. The platform employs security features, including two-factor authentication and encryption, to protect user data and funds. Understanding these security measures is essential for users, especially those new to trading, as they navigate the complexities of online investing. Furthermore, Robinhood provides information on how it safeguards users against unauthorized access, helping to instill confidence in its clients. As users become more aware of these security protocols, they can make informed investment decisions and feel more secure using the app.

Trading financial instruments and cryptocurrencies through Robinhood has become increasingly popular, mainly as the app offers a seamless experience for users. Individuals can trade stocks, options, ETFs, and even cryptocurrencies like Bitcoin and Ethereum with a few taps. This ease of access to diverse financial products empowers users to build their investment portfolios to align with their financial goals. Beginner traders can take advantage of educational resources within the app, which guides them through the trading process, helping them to develop effective strategies and understand market dynamics.

Regarding financial guarantees, Robinhood provides users with protections that align with industry standards, including SIPC insurance for securities and cash. This coverage offers protection, ensuring that users' investments are safeguarded in case of brokerage failure. Understanding these guarantees is crucial for users as they assess the risks associated with trading. Robinhood's transparent policies regarding fund transfers to and from ACH accounts also streamline the process, making it easier for users to manage their finances effectively and maintain liquidity for trading activities.

Looking ahead, the future developments of the Robinhood app promise to enhance the user experience further and expand its capabilities. Innovations in trading technology, such as advanced analytics tools and personalized investment recommendations, are on the horizon, which could empower users to make more informed decisions. As the financial landscape continues to evolve, Robinhood aims to stay at the forefront by integrating features that cater to the changing needs of investors. For beginners embarking on their investment journey, staying informed about these advancements will be essential in maximizing their potential for success in the dynamic world of trading.

www.ingramcontent.com/pod-product-compliance
Lightning Source LLC
LaVergne TN
LVHW090334210926
848480LV00004B/1402
* 9 7 9 8 2 3 0 5 8 3 4 5 5 *